Freud
FOR BEGINNERS

Richard Appignanesi and Oscar Zarate

This edition published in 1992 by Icon Books Ltd.,
Cavendish House, Cambridge Road, Barton, Cambridge.

Text copyright © 1979 Richard Appignanesi
Illustrations copyright © 1979 Oscar Zarate

The author and artist have their moral rights.

A CIP catalogue record for this book is available from the British Library

ISBN 1 874166 00 5

Printed and bound in Great Britain by
BPCC Hazells Ltd

Member of BPCC Ltd

FREUD FOR BEGINNERS

6 MAY 1856: Sigmund Freud is born in Freiburg, Moravia, which is today in Czechoslovakia but was then part of the Austro-Hungarian Empire. Freud's ancestry was Jewish.

HIS FATHER, **JAKOB FREUD** (1815-96), WAS A FAIRLY SUCCESSFUL WOOL MERCHANT. JAKOB WAS 40, WITH TWO GROWN SONS AND ALREADY A GRANDFATHER, WHEN HE WAS MARRIED, FOR A SECOND TIME, TO **AMALIE NATHANSON** (1835-1930). SIGI WAS THE FIRST — AND FAVOURITE — OF AMALIE'S 8 CHILDREN.

1860: the Freud family moves permanently to Vienna, the ancient capital of the Hapsburg Empire. Freud's choice of boyhood heroes reveals a deep dislike of Imperial Vienna: the anti-monarchist **Oliver Cromwell** and the Carthaginian general **Hannibal.**

WHY HANNIBAL, SON?

BECAUSE HE WAS A **SEMITIC** LEADER WHO FOUGHT THE ROMANS!

AND AUSTRIA WAS ROMAN CATHOLIC AND ANTI-SEMITIC.

7

Vienna in the 1890s was famous for its Blue Danube, its wit, sensuality, waltzes and cafés . . . But it had a **darker** side!

POVERTY

The Empire was in deep economic trouble. The jobless were crowded in slums and flophouses.

RACISM
Karl Lueger, Mayor of Vienna, made anti-Semitism politically fashionable.

PROSTITUTION, DISEASE, SEXUAL HYPOCRISY

The brighter side:
Social improvement was the bright hope of Social Democracy — the Austrian brand of parliamentary Marxism.

1873: Freud begins medical studies at the University of Vienna and finishes in 1881 — three years longer than normal. Freud's special interests are histology and neurophysiology: the scientific study of organic tissues and the nervous system. He wanted to be a **scientist** — not a doctor.

ONE OF FREUD'S TEACHERS, **ERNST BRÜCKE (1819-92),** THE GREAT GERMAN PHYSIOLOGIST, WAS A FOUNDER OF **MECHANISM.**

THE LEADING MECHANIST, **HERMANN HELMHOLTZ** (1821-94).

THE SO-CALLED VITAL FUNCTIONS ARE SIMPLY EXCHANGES OF ENERGY BETWEEN LIVING AND NONLIVING MATTER.

A NERVOUS IMPULSE TRAVELS ALONG THE NERVE FIBRE OF A FROG AT 50 FEET PER SECOND.

Mechanism proposed that 'life' should be investigated and understood by the experimental methods of chemistry and physics.

1876-81: Freud does important pioneering work on nerve cells.

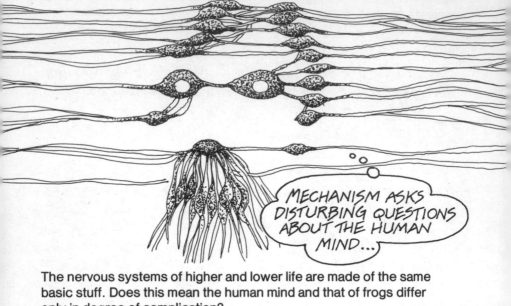

MECHANISM ASKS DISTURBING QUESTIONS ABOUT THE HUMAN MIND...

The nervous systems of higher and lower life are made of the same basic stuff. Does this mean the human mind and that of frogs differ only in degree of complication?
The Mechanist answer is — yes!

1882: Freud was happy doing scientific work at Brücke's University lab. But Brücke gave him some fatherly advice . . .

ACADEMIC POSTS ARE FEW AND BADLY PAID. YOUR CHANCES OF ADVANCEMENT AS A JEW ARE **BAD.**

MY FATHER CAN'T AFFORD TO SUPPORT ME. THE CRASH OF 1873 RUINED HIM... AND HE HAS 6 OTHER CHILDREN TO FEED!

There was something else — marriage plans. Freud met and fell in love with **Martha Bernays** (1861-1951).

1882-1885: Freud had to face another long training period in clinical medicine at the Vienna General Hospital before starting a private practice.

First he served as assistant to **Hermann Nothnagel** (1841-1905), Professor of Internal Medicine.

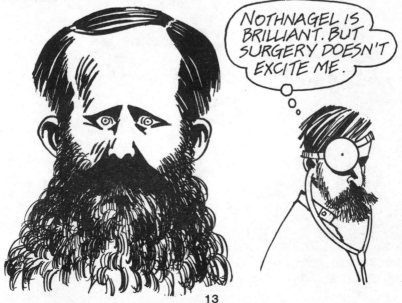

1883: Freud spends 5 months working in the Psychiatric Clinic under **Theodor Meynert** (1833-92), the greatest brain anatomist and neuropathologist at that time.

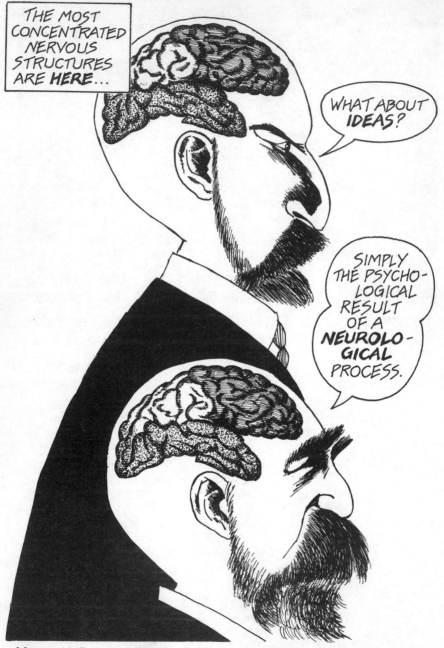

Meynert influenced Freud to become a specialist in neuropathology (diseases of the nervous system).

1884-87: Freud studied the effects of **cocaine** — starting on himself.
Freud even prescribed it to Martha!

Freud's close friend, the gifted physiologist **Ernst von Fleischl-Marxow** (1846-91), suffered from a painful tumour of the hand.

COCAINE IS AN ANTI-DEPRESSANT, A HARMLESS ANAESTHETIC.

I'VE BECOME A MORPHINE ADDICT...

WHY NOT TRY COCAINE INSTEAD?

In 1885 Freud assisted his colleagues Carl Koller and Leopold Koenigstein in a successful operation on Jakob Freud's eye. Cocaine was applied as a local anaesthetic.

Carl Koller put in his claim first as the discoverer of cocaine.

Why? Because by 1886 cases of cocaine addiction were reported everywhere.

And Fleischl-Marxow had become a despairing addict.

1885-86: 19 WEEKS WITH CHARCOT

Freud was awarded a small grant to study in Paris with **Jean Martin Charcot** (1825-93) world-famous neurologist and director of the Salpêtrière asylum.

But what exactly is **hysteria**?
1. The Greek word **hystera** means womb or uterus.
2. It was believed only **women** could suffer hysterical symptoms: paralysis, convulsions, somnambulism, hallucinations, loss of speech, sensations or memory.
3. Hysterics were once persecuted as **witches**.

Specialists had 2 radically different views:
1. either hysteria is an 'irritation' of the female sexual organs treated by pressure on the ovaries, packing them in ice, and surgical attacks on the clitoris,
2. or hysteria is imaginary, mere play-acting by women.

Charcot rejects the traditional diagnosis

18

Hysteria baffled doctors because the symptoms were apparently not caused by any **physical** damage.
For instance . . .

But genuine paralysis caused, say, by a stroke is not so **precise** as that. It will 'shade off' a little to the face, or leg, etc.

Charcot demonstrated a startling resemblance between hysteria and **hypnotism.** Hypnotic suggestion could be used to induce hysterical symptoms — such as paralysis.

Hysteria can only develop where there is hereditary **degeneration of the brain.**

20

Charcot was a good Mechanist: explanations had to be strictly **physical.**

Charcot prevented Freud from asking **psychological** questions. Charcot's view that hysteria was not connected to the female sexual organs was an **advance,** yes. But it stopped Freud from asking whether some mental disorders might have a **sexual origin.**

April 1886: Freud begins private practice as a neuropathologist and encounters his first hysterics.

EXAMINATION SHOWS NO EVIDENCE OF STRUCTURAL DAMAGE...

EITHER I CAN SAY, "PULL YOURSELF TOGETHER."...

OR USE ELECTRO-THERAPY.*

*LOCAL ELECTRICAL STIMULATION OF SKIN AND MUSCLES—NOT SHOCK THERAPY, DISCOVERED YEARS LATER.

15 Oct. 1886: Freud reads his paper on **Male Hysteria** before the Vienna Medical Society.

Freud was still a convinced Mechanist. His first scientific book was on brain-damage which affects language ability, **Aphasia** (1891), his next **Infantile Cerebral Paralysis** (1891-93).

A new theory of hypnotism, developed at Nancy, France, challenged Charcot's views.

Someone else in Vienna had experimented with hypnotism: an old friend of Freud's and respected physician, **Josef Breuer** (1842-1925). Back in 1882 Breuer had told Freud about an interesting case of hysteria.

THE CASE OF ANNA O

An intelligent woman of 21. A strict upbringing left her sexually immature.
In July 1880 Anna's father fell seriously ill . . .

I NURSED HIM DAY AND NIGHT TILL I COLLAPSED EXHAUSTED IN DECEMBER...

WHEN I WAS CALLED IN.

HER SYMPTOMS WERE A SEVERE NERVOUS COUGH, A SQUINT, VISUAL DISTURBANCES AND...

...PARALYSIS OF THE RIGHT ARM AND NECK. AND A STRANGE SPEECH PROBLEM.

SHE COULD UNDERSTAND WHEN SPOKEN TO IN GERMAN. BUT OFTEN SHE REPLIED IN ENGLISH.

SHE WAS AGITATED BY HALLUCINATIONS.

MY 'NAUGHTY STATES'...

AT FIRST SHE SEEMED TO IMPROVE. UNTIL APRIL 1881 WHEN HER FATHER DIED. HER HALLUCINATIONS...

...BECAME MORE VIOLENT DURING THE DAYTIME.

BUT IN THE EVENINGS SHE FELL INTO A QUIET TRANCE AND MUMBLED WORDS TO HERSELF.

ONE OF THESE WAS **HYDROPHOBIA**. FOR 6 WEEKS ANNA WAS UNABLE TO DRINK ANY LIQUID.

JUST RAISING THE GLASS DISGUSTS ME!

BUT DURING ONE OF HER TRANCES...

IN AN ENGLISHWOMAN'S ROOM, ONE DAY, I SAW HER DOG DRINKING WATER FROM A GLASS. HOW DISGUSTING! POLITENESS FORBADE ME TO SAY ANYTHING...

BUT NOW?

NOW I **CAN** SAY IT! THAT **AWFUL** WOMAN, THAT **HORRIBLE** DOG!

AND WHEN SHE CAME OUT OF HER TRANCE...

I'D FORGOTTEN THAT DOG UNTIL NOW!

H'M, INTERESTING!

I DECIDED FROM NOW ON TO HYPNOTIZE ANNA DELIBERATELY.

1.
Each symptom disappeared when traced back to its first occasion.

2.
Symptoms were removed by recalling forgotten unpleasant events.

3.
A symptom emerged with greatest force when it was being talked away.

BREUER BEGAN TO APPLY HIS DISCOVERIES.

CAN YOU RECALL HOW YOU STARTED TO SQUINT?

...I WAS UPSET AND WANTED TO CRY... BUT I WAS AFRAID MY TEARS WOULD ALARM HIM...

WHAT TIME IS IT?

FREUD TOLD CHARCOT ABOUT THE CASE.

HE WASN'T IMPRESSED.

SO FREUD DIDN'T THINK OF USING BREUER'S **CATHARTIC METHOD** TILL 1889.

YOU KNOW, ANNA FALLING IN LOVE WITH YOU? THAT NEEDS EXAMINING!

BUT **NOT** BY ME, THANKS!

Anna's real name was **Bertha Pappenheim** (1859-1936). She recovered and became a leading social worker and feminist.

COMMEMORATED ON A STAMP

Freud had to persuade a very reluctant Breuer to work jointly on a book:
STUDIES IN HYSTERIA (1895)

Some key ideas and terms
Freud and Breuer concluded that: "Hysterics suffer mainly from reminiscences."
This means:
1. Hysterics suffer from painful, unpleasant memories of a **traumatic** nature (**trauma**, Greek for 'wound').
2. Traumatic memories are **pathogenic**, disease-creating. This was a revolutionary anti-mechanist notion which implied that a psychical (strictly **mental**) agent directly influences the physical processes of the body.
3. Traumatic memories do not 'wear away' normally but remain an active and **unconscious** force motivating behaviour. (What cannot be remembered cannot be left behind.)
4. Banishment of painful, emotionally-charged memories from consciousness requires an active **repressing** mechanism operating at an unconscious level of mental life.
5. Since negative, unconscious memories cannot be expressed normally, their emotional energy or **affect** is dammed up — strangulated.
6. The strangulated affect is 'converted' into the physical symptoms of hysteria by unconscious stimulus.
7. Symptoms stimulated by the unconscious will disappear if **abreaction** occurs. Abreaction is the process of releasing a repressed emotion about a previously forgotten event. The problem of therapy is to get the patient to relive the original traumatic experience which caused the symptom.
8. Therapy will be difficult because every symptom is **over-determined**. It is caused by, and is the characteristic of, **several** psychological events.

THE IDEAS THEY RESIST USUALLY TURN OUT TO BE **SEXUAL**!

I THINK WE CAN STOP SOON...

OH NOT YET!

YOU MEAN...

YES! YOU SHOULD HAVE TREATED ANNA'S LOVE AS ONE MORE **SUBSTITUTE** SYMPTOM – AND DISCOVERED THE SEXUAL BASIS OF HER ILLNESS!

CAN STOP SOON...

MAYBE. BUT I CAN'T AGREE WITH YOU.

H'M... BREUER **RESISTS** THE IDEA TOO!

Freud's early theory of a sexual cause disturbed Breuer and led to a split between them.

36

1892-96: THE PRESSURE TECHNIQUE
For the first time Freud uses a couch. He presses his hand on the patient's forehead and asks questions.

"MY SISTER AND I SHARED A *SECRET* - WE SLEPT IN ONE ROOM ... AND ONE NIGHT A MAN SEXUALLY ASSAULTED US! "

THE SEDUCTION THEORY

Repeated experiences with patients led Freud to propose a seduction theory.

1. Repressed memories nearly always revealed seduction or sexual molestation by a parent or adult.
2. This traumatic event in childhood operates in a delayed way. The repressed memory becomes a pathogenic idea which can cause hysterical symptoms after puberty.

1896: FREUD COINS THE TERM
PSYCHOANALYSIS

THE 'PRESSURE' TECHNIQUE HAS TO GIVE WAY TOO.

THE FREE ASSOCIATION TECHNIQUE
Patients must be free, without censorship or urging . . .

AN IMPORTANT HUMAN ADVANCE

1. Charcot took a first step towards a more 'human' treatment of neuroses.
2. But hypnosis, and even the pressure technique, were still arbitrary and authoritarian.
3. The free association technique of recalling traumatic events was completely new and revolutionary.
   The clue to neurotic symptoms is hidden in the patient's unconscious. The patient doesn't know what's repressed in the unconscious. And yet, **only** the patient can lead the therapist to its discovery and relief.
   Both the patient and the doctor must search.
4. However, the patient will resist and be less able to cooperate as the unpleasant material emerges. Then the doctor's clinical experience becomes important.
5. Patience in following a neurotic's blind wanderings must be justified, because resistance is only an attempt to postpone the emergence of the repressed material. No matter how roundabout, all routes must be connected with it.

The only person willing to listen to Freud was **Wilhelm Fliess** (1858-1928), a Berlin nose-and-throat specialist. They met fairly often and exchanged many letters between 1893 and 1902.

BUT FLIESS HAD SOME PRETTY STRANGE THEORIES!

ILLNESSES—ESPECIALLY SEXUAL ONES—ARE CAUSED BY DISTURBANCES IN THE MUCOUS MEMBRANES OF THE NOSE.

FLIESS OPERATED ON FREUD TWICE FOR NASAL INFECTIONS.

NOTHING SEXUAL—OF COURSE!

!

IMAGINE WHAT HE'D DO TO CYRANO DE BERGERAC!

FLIESS DIAGNOSED FREUD AGAIN... BREUER DISAGREED.

HEART DISEASE DUE TO NICOTINE POISONING!

I CAN'T FIND ANYTHING SERIOUS.

TO KEEP **THINKING** I'VE GOT TO KEEP SMOKING!

I KEEP HAVING THESE TERRIBLE MIGRAINES...

AND MY IDEAS COME SLOWLY AFTER **MUCH** AGONY AND DOUBT!

BUT THE WORST THING IS MY **TODESANGST** (DEATH ANXIETY)

FROM THE OUTSIDE FREUD SEEMED IN COMPLETE CONTROL. HIS ONE AMBITION WAS **SCIENCE**.

BUT HE ALWAYS HAD TIME FOR HIS CHILDREN.

AT 40 FREUD HAD 6 CHILDREN, A WIFE, PARENTS AND SISTERS TO SUPPORT...

AND MY THEORIES DIDN'T ADD UP TO MUCH FINANCIALLY!

HIS RELAXATIONS WERE FEW: A SATURDAY EVENING GAME OF CARDS, COUNTRY WALKS, MUSHROOM HUNTING AND COLLECTING ANTIQUITIES.

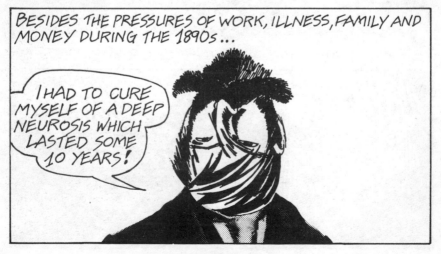

BESIDES THE PRESSURES OF WORK, ILLNESS, FAMILY AND MONEY DURING THE 1890s...

I HAD TO CURE MYSELF OF A DEEP NEUROSIS WHICH LASTED SOME 10 YEARS!

23 Oct. 1896: Freud's father dies.
During this period of crisis and self-analysis Freud begins writing
The Interpretation of Dreams.

One of Freud's own dreams from **THE INTERPRETATION OF DREAMS** (1900):

Freud in a train station is accompanied by an 'elderly gentleman.'
"I think of a plan for remaining disguised. But that seems to have happened already!"
The old man seems blind — perhaps in one eye. Freud hands him a male glass urinal. "So I'm his nurse!" And here the old man's attitude and his penis appear in clear form. At this point Freud awoke feeling a need to urinate.

How does Freud interpret his dream?
I remember an embarrassing event in my parent's bedroom when I was
7 or 8 . . .

What a terrible blow to my **ambition** !

In fact, bed-wetting and the character trait of ambition are linked in
some cases of neurosis.

This childhood insult to my ambition provided material for a dream in
adult life. As if I wanted to say, "You see, I have amounted to
something!"

The old blind man is my father. Blindness refers to his eye operation,
my discovery of cocaine and his operation. That is one wish fulfilled.
Another is the hostile wish to put my father in a defenceless position, as
I was in childhood, to **shame** him. The 'disguise' refers to my
discoveries about hysteria, of which I felt proud.

Another childhood remembrance: on the train journey from Leipzig in 1860 I saw my mother naked.

Several years later I had an anxiety dream . . .
My mother, with a strangely peaceful, sleeping expression on her face, was carried into the room by some bird-headed people and laid upon the bed.
I awoke screaming and ran to my parents.

FREUD'S INTERPRETATION

I had seen those bird-headed gods from Egyptian funerary sculpture in Philippson's Bible. And a boy called Philipp told me the slang word for sex. **Vögeln,** the German slang for sex, also means birds.

My mother's "peaceful" look I transferred from my grandfather as he lay dying. My anxiety over her "death" disguises a wish directed against my father.

This dream contains a typical childhood wish: a **death wish** aimed at the father and a **sexual** one at the mother.

Does the idea seem repugnant? Consider the myths and legends of ancient cultures.

Saturn devoured his children out of fear that they might overthrow him as king of the gods.
Zeus castrated his father, Saturn, and took his place.

And ask yourself . . . Why is there a Fifth Commandment?

NOW CONSIDER THIS PATIENT OF MINE— AN OBSESSIONAL NEUROTIC.

AN OBSESSIONAL NEUROTIC

AND HIS WISH REALLY GOES BACK TO CHILDHOOD!

THIS REMINDED FREUD OF THE ANCIENT GREEK LEGEND OF *OEDIPUS.*

THE OEDIPUS STORY

KING LAIUS OF THEBES AND QUEEN JOCASTA ARE
WARNED BY A PROPHET...

YOUR CHILD WILL
GROW UP TO MURDER
HIS FATHER AND
MARRY HIS MOTHER!

AT BIRTH THE INFANT'S
FEET ARE PIERCED
(OEDIPUS'S 'SWOLLEN FOOT'),
AND HE IS LEFT IN THE
MOUNTAINS TO DIE.

RESCUED BY SHEPHERDS,
OEDIPUS GROWS UP AS THE SON
OF A FOREIGN KING AND QUEEN.

OEDIPUS IS MADE KING OF THEBES AND MARRIES JOCASTA.

KING OEDIPUS REIGNS IN PEACE - UNTIL A PLAGUE BREAKS OUT AND A PROPHET IS AGAIN CONSULTED.

THE PLAGUE WILL END ONLY *IF* THE MURDERER OF LAIUS IS DISCOVERED!

BUT **WHO** IS THE GUILTY ONE?

OEDIPUS BLINDS HIMSELF WHEN HE DISCOVERS HIS 'UNCONSCIOUS' CRIME. JOCASTA COMMITS SUICIDE.

BLINDING IS SYMBOLIC OF THE HORROR WHICH FOLLOWS THE REVELATION OF REPRESSED IDEAS OR WISHES.

WHY IS THIS STORY OF OEDIPUS SO FASCINATING?

BECAUSE OEDIPUS ACTS OUT A WISH THAT EVERYONE HAS HAD IN EARLY CHILDHOOD!

THIS INCEST FANTASY - FALLING IN LOVE WITH THE MOTHER, JEALOUSY OF THE FATHER - IS WHAT FREUD LATER CALLED THE **OEDIPUS COMPLEX.**

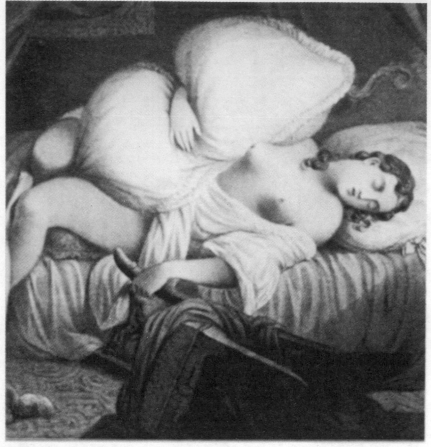

Freud's **The Interpretation of Dreams** contains 2 revolutionary discoveries:

1. The solution to the meaning of dreams — generally that "all dreams represent the fulfilment of wishes."
2. The functioning of dreams provides systematic evidence of the unconscious.

First, let's see how dreams work.

Dreams occur during sleep — when the conscious part of personality is most relaxed and off-guard.

Dreaming is perfectly normal.

Wish-fulfilments in dreams are usually (but not always) sexual.

Although dreams express wishes, this doesn't mean you can dream anything you "wish"!

The wish is often so well hidden, disguised or distorted, that you might not realize a sexual wish has even appeared in your dream.

LET'S LOOK AT A SIMPLE EXAMPLE.

A PATIENT OF MINE DREAMED THAT SOMEONE GAVE HER A COMB...

I COULDN'T SEE WHO IT WAS... BUT HE WANTED TO HAND ME A COMB.

THE PART YOU REMEMBER IS CALLED THE **MANIFEST CONTENT** OF THE DREAM.

CAN WE FIND OUT WHAT IT MEANS?

ONLY IF WE CAN GET BACK TO THE **LATENT CONTENT,** WHICH CONTAINS YOUR REPRESSED UNCONSCIOUS WISH.

WHERE DO WE START?

FIRST WITH YOUR PAST HISTORY...

So even in this simple example we see that:
1. Dreams are only a partial or censored expression of a wish.
2. The latent content of the dream (which contains the unconscious sexual wish) is only allowed to appear if it is disguised as manifest content.

The manifest content appears like a coded message, a scrambled or censored jigsaw puzzle.

The manifest dream is forced to express the latent idea by using **symbols** — all kinds of objects which normally don't have any sexual meaning at all.

These disguised images of latent ideas have become popularly known as "Freudian symbols."

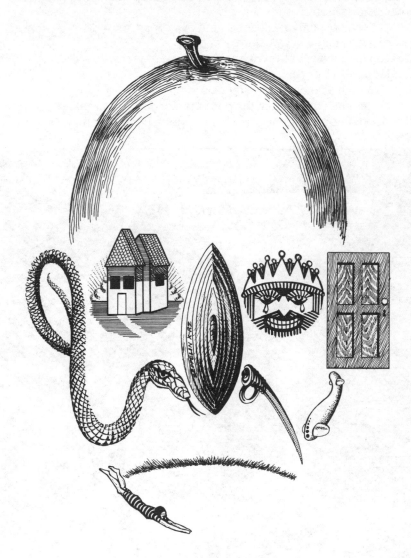

Any manifest object which suggests penetration, such as swords, guns, umbrellas, snakes, etc., can symbolize the penis.
Objects suggesting receptacles, such as boxes, purses, caves, etc., can symbolize the vagina.
But Freud warns that interpretation is never so simple.

Freud said that dreaming functions like a miniature model of neurosis. But if dreaming is normal, why should it provide a clue to neurotic behavior?

Let's retrace some of the steps which first gave Freud the evidence of unconscious ideas.

We've seen how the manifest content of a dream expresses a latent sexual wish indirectly by using symbols.

This "shifting over" of the wish to a manifest object was called **displacement** by Freud.

Displacement also occurs in neurosis.

The emotional energy from the pathogenic (disease-creating) idea is displaced onto symptoms. And this happens unconsciously.

This brings us to Freud's second discovery, which revolutionized our picture of the human mind.

THE UNCONSCIOUS

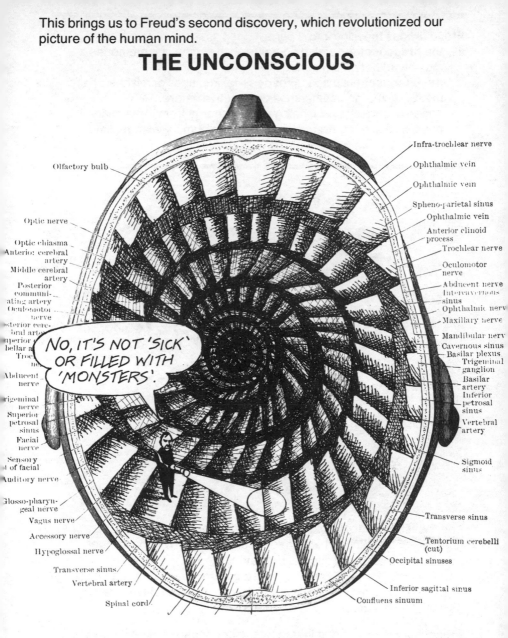

Freud wasn't interested only in the "sick" mind, as is often supposed. What he gave us was a general theory of the mind.

Neuroses aren't simple diseased abnormalities — but rather another sort of mental functioning.

However, neuroses allow glimpses into the hidden depths of the mind which aren't "normally" open to inspection.

Freud divides the mind into 2 parts:

1. the **preconscious** which contains all the ideas and memories capable of becoming conscious
2. the **unconscious** made up of desires, impulses or wishes of a mostly sexual and sometimes destructive nature.
   These unconscious wishes get their energy from the primary physical instincts. Freud also called this primary wish-fulfilment drive by another name . . .

THE PLEASURE PRINCIPLE

The Pleasure Principle can easily run into conflict with the conscious activities of the mind, which are concerned with avoiding danger, adapting to reality and civilized behaviour.
Preconsciousness operates in a more controlled, disciplined "thinking" manner. It takes the demands of reality into account and tolerates delays of satisfaction.

Preconsciousness is dominated by the secondary process or what Freud also called . . .

THE REALITY PRINCIPLE

Freud once said that the highest civilized form of the Reality Principle is . . . **SCIENCE**.

What happens when the mind is dominated by the primary wish-fulfilment process or the Pleasure Principle?

Let's take a nonsexual example: a hungry man lost in a forest without food.

If the primary idea of "food" takes him over, he won't be able to think of ways of getting food.

But if the secondary process, or Reality Principle, gains control, he can "forget" food long enough to consider how to obtain it.

The primary wish-fulfilment ideas which dominate the unconscious are impulsive, unorganized and don't obey any logic.

So, according to Freud, all human thought is partly a conflict, partly a compromise between the preconscious and unconscious systems.

FREUD FORGETS TO REMEMBER ...

I'VE RUN OUT OF **LOSCHPAPIER** .∴. I MUST REMEMBER TO GET SOME IN TOWN.

* BLOTTING-PAPER IN ENGLISH

BUT FOR MANY DAYS RUNNING FREUD KEPT **FORGETTING** ...

WHY, I WONDER? BECAUSE USUALLY I ASK FOR **FLIESSPAPIER !** *

* ANOTHER TERM FOR BLOTTING-PAPER

...AND MY FRIENDSHIP WITH **FLIESS** IS BREAKING UP. SO THIS PAINFUL ASSOCIATIVE **THOUGHT** IS MANIFESTED BY FORGETTING !

Freud's book THE PSYCHOPATHOLOGY OF EVERYDAY LIFE (1901) describes other typical examples of 'forgetting.' **Parapraxis** is the official term for the famous 'Freudian slip.' It refers to slips of the tongue, pen or memory, which occur in **normal** life.
Errors are symbolic of unconscious attitudes and wishes.
There are no errors in the **mind**!

In 1905 Freud published his **THREE ESSAYS ON THE THEORY OF SEXUALITY.**

The simple enjoyment of sex isn't so simple.
What is the conventional view of sex?

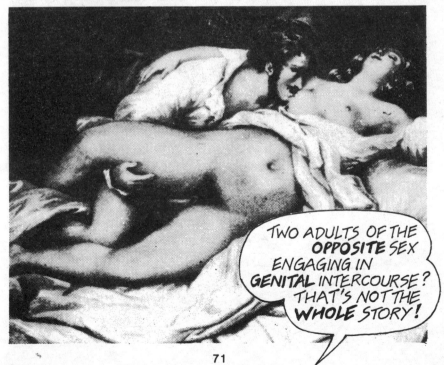

1. persons only attracted by their **own** sex or their **own** genitals?
2. persons known as 'perverts' who disregard the normal use of sex?
These facts are known but not admitted as **normal.**

Freud overturns the conventional view of sex and perversion:
1. The aims of pleasure and **procreation** do not coincide completely.
2. 'Sexual' and 'genital' are two very different concepts.
3. Sexual pleasure can be obtained from any part or zone of the body.
4. Sexuality includes urges not related to genital activity. The normal 'foreplay' uses of mouth, touch, etc., are the **component instincts** of sexuality.

But if such instincts are not in themselves 'perverse,' what actually defines perversion?

SUPPOSE A **SINGLE** COMPONENT INSTINCT BECOMES HIGHLY SEXUALIZED? SUPPOSE IT **REPLACES** THE NORMAL SEXUAL AIM?

WELL, YOU GET TYPICAL EXAMPLES OF SEXUAL DEVIANCE... **THE VOYEUR** (LOOKING)

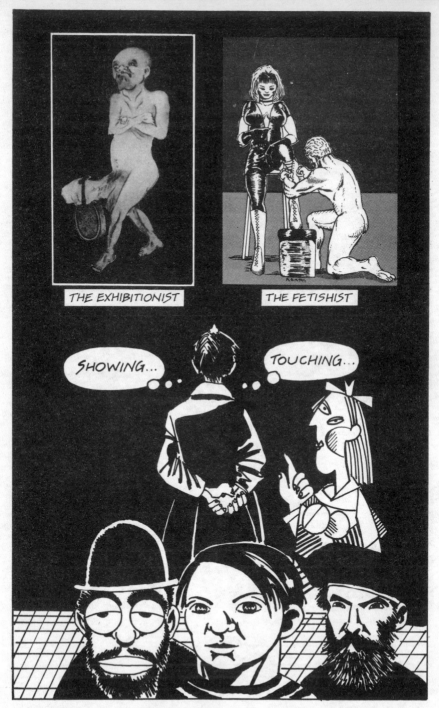

THE EXHIBITIONIST

THE FETISHIST

SHOWING...

TOUCHING...

NORMAL FOLKS **PARTLY** SATISFY SUCH URGES IN THEIR SEX LIFE AND DREAMS.

This neurotic resistance to wishful 'perverse' urges is what led Freud back to **childhood** sexuality.

GOING BACK TO CHILDHOOD

Everyone is born with a basic sex drive, or instinctual energy, called the LIBIDO (Latin for 'desire').

The sex drive has both mental and physical features.

These features are:

1. an internal organic **source** of excitation
2. a quantity or **pressure** of excitation
3. an **aim,** which is to achieve a sensation of pleasure by removing the pressure
4. an **object,** which is a thing or person in reality required to satisfy the aim.

THE SEXUAL HISTORY OF THE INDIVIDUAL BEGINS AT BIRTH

Which means it takes sexual pleasure from the stimulation of **any** part of its body.

Acquiring specific **aim** and **object** needs experience: a complex learning process which can easily "go wrong."

The specific organs of sexual satisfaction are established on the basis of the EROTOGENIC ZONES.

This primary Oral Stage can also be understood in a wider historical sense. It appears again in adult fantasy, in mythology and the history of culture.

For example, the loss of the oral love-object reminds us of a famous mythological loss.

THE FALL FROM PARADISE

BECAUSE OF AN ORAL SIN!

But there is also an old cultural wish to REGAIN PARADISE.
This painting by Brueghel (1567) shows us Utopia, the earthly paradise of perfect oral pleasure.

SECOND ZONE: THE ANAL STAGE

THE EXCREMENTAL FUNCTION IS BOUND UP WITH SOCIAL IDEAS OF ORDER, CLEANLINESS - AND DISGUST.

These anal ideas of gift, skill, creation, blame and restrictive order again remind us of another great cultural myth.

PROMETHEUS: THE ORIGINATOR OF HUMAN CIVILIZATION

Prometheus the Titan:
1. made the first humans out of mud (a substance like excrement)
2. gave humans their first great gift, fire, and taught them the first skills
3. was punished by the gods who chained him to a rock and sent an eagle to peck at his guts.

THIRD ZONE: THE PHALLIC STAGE

BY THE AGE OF 3 OR 4 CHILDREN DISCOVER **THE THING** TO BE CREATIVE WITH. MASTURBATION, STIMULATION OF THE GENITAL ZONE, COMES NATURALLY, BUT...

Note:

The concept 'phallic' is not exclusively masculine. It applies at this stage to infants of **both** sexes.

Infants of both genders believe they can either give their mothers a child, or produce one themselves anally.

Curiosity, anxiety and confusion about **differences** of sexual anatomy now begin.

And the child at 5 or 6 enters the OEDIPUS COMPLEX phase, as the following case shows.

THE CASE OF LITTLE HANS (1909)

HANS BECAME INTERESTED IN HIS PENIS – AND HIS FATHER'S.

MASTURBATION WAS 'TYPICALLY' DISCOURAGED.

84

What about the girls? Is their Oedipal phase the same as boys'?

Both boys and girls at first assume they have phallic power of some sort
— and mother is their incestuous love-object.
But desiring Mum brings up fears of Dad!
This, as in Hans's case, leads boys to **castration anxiety.**

But what does a girl discover? That she is **already** castrated . . .

The girl's discovery that neither she nor her mother possesses a penis
is **real.** It is not like the boy's fantasy-fear of being castrated.
She can feel hostile and reproach her mother for bringing her into the
world "in this shape."

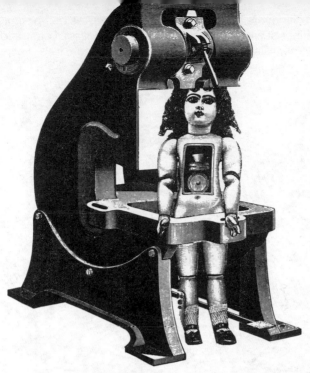

So while the boys develop castration anxiety, girls instead develop what Freud called **penis envy.**

The girl's sexual development branches off from the boy's and takes a more complex path.

When the girl discovers she is in the "same shape" as her mother, her repression of incest wishes need not depend on fears of castration (like the boy's) and her relation to her father may now seem free . . .

The "Oedipal riddle" confronts both sexes on the way to adult sexuality.

The path to healthy, mature female sexuality means:
1. accepting the **idea** of union with a male
2. leaving the father behind after adolescent emancipation
3. coming to terms with the mother.

The question of sexual development isn't simple.
Freud was always aware of the **two-sided** nature of both sexes — in other words, BISEXUALITY.
1. Freud observed that in human beings **pure** masculinity or femininity does not exist in a psychological or a biological sense.
2. Every individual shows masculine **and** feminine character traits.

Freud was aware that social customs force women into passive roles which are supposed to be "really feminine."

Freud kept developing his theory of female sexuality.
Here's how he ended a lecture on femininity in 1933:
"What I've had to say about femininity doesn't always sound friendly. It is incomplete. If you want to know **more,** look at your own experience of life . . ."

...OR WAIT UNTIL SCIENCE CAN GIVE YOU DEEPER INFORMATION!

Women in psychology have long been rethinking and developing Freud's theories: Lou Andreas-Salomé, Anna Freud, Marie Bonaparte, Helene Deutsch, Karen Horney, Melanie Klein, Clara Thompson, Juliet Mitchell, and many others.

4. THE LATENCY STAGE

From about the age of 6 until puberty, the sex drive seems to disappear.

It goes underground. Infantile amnesia takes place: so total that people can later deny their earliest sexual experiences.

The infantile stage of sexuality ends with the **repression** of the Oedipus Complex.

Ideas and impulses associated with the oral, anal and phallic stages are pushed into the unconscious (i.e. **repressed**) and denied expression.

But the impulses are still there — in latent form, as the structure the libido has acquired. The sexually organized memories of the 3 stages will influence future associations.

Sexuality returns in adolescence with the problem of physical capacity for sex!

In animals the sex instinct is **pre-adapted** to reality. It is biologically **fixed.**

"Only in humans does sexual life occur in two waves, in infancy and at puberty. Something that is unknown except in humans and evidently has an important bearing on **hominization**."

We are normal (psychologically healthy) when our quest for knowledge is **uninhibited.**

What are neurotics 'ignorant' of? Something **prevents** them from knowing what's causing their misery. Or, as Freud would say, they are victims of **unconscious inhibitions.** Inhibition simply means a **restraint** against knowing the origin of the problem which determines the neurotic's rigid pattern of behaviour.

Freud traces the origin of neurotic problems back to childhood.
Something can go wrong in the learning process — in the way the
structure of human sexual instinct is acquired.

Here's what happens:
1. **Fixation** (arrested development) of the libido may occur at a
   particular childhood stage (oral, anal, Oedipal).
2. **Regression** (a return) to this early "fixated" level can take place,
   leading to various forms of adult neuroses.
Neurotics are literally in "a fix," in "a bind." **Anal fixation**, for instance,
shows up in all sorts of inhibited behaviour.

the miser   **obsession with order**   **uncompleted tasks**

Consciously the miser obsesses about keeping his money. But
unconsciously he is "holding on" to the symbolic value associated with
excrement at the childhood anal stage.
Obsessive ideas are ones which persist despite being incompatible
with the conscious part of personality.

96

For the fetishist, a shoe or fur or part of the body will take the place of human relationship entirely.

Another form of incomplete maturity of the sexual aim or object is **inversion** (the "turning in" of the libido on to an object like oneself) commonly known as homosexuality.

Sexual development often can "go wrong." This led Freud to a revolutionary new idea.

Normal sexuality is only one way of ending up. It is acquired from many components which can split off and become fixated.

Freud's theory of sexuality made him world famous . . . for the wrong reasons!

The hostility is understandable. Freud struck the **third revolutionary blow** to human pride.

1ˢᵗ REVOLUTION
(COSMOLOGY)

THE EARTH (AND THEREFORE HUMANITY) IS **NOT** AT THE CENTRE OF THE UNIVERSE.

COPERNICUS
(1473-1543)

MOON

EARTH

FIXED STARS

2ᴺᴰ REVOLUTION
(BIOLOGY)

MAN IS NOT GOD'S CREATION BUT AN EVOLVED APE.

DARWIN
(1809-1882)

100

FREUD'S 3rd REVOLUTION: THE PSYCHOLOGY OF THE UNCONSCIOUS

Philosophers have always equated mind with consciousness. But Freud said something else. Only a small part of what is mental is conscious. The rest is **unconscious**, made up of inadmissible and involuntary ideas which motivate behaviour.

YOU MEAN THE HUMAN MIND IS IRRATIONAL?

I MEAN REASON IS NOT SOMETHING GIVEN. IT HAS TO BE STRUGGLED FOR!

LAST SUMMER A FELLOW-OFFICER TOLD ME ABOUT A CHINESE TORTURE...
A POT IS FILLED WITH RATS AND TIED UPSIDE-DOWN ON THE VICTIM'S BUTTOCKS. THE RATS THEN GNAW THEIR WAY OUT THROUGH THE ANUS...

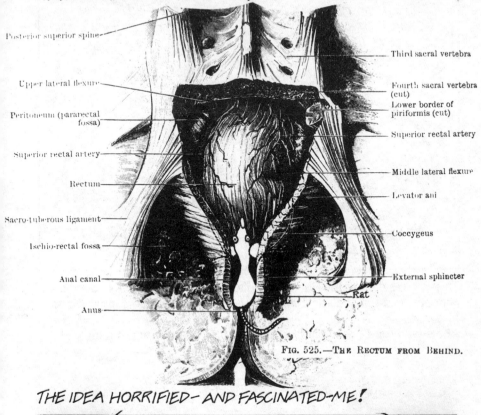

Posterior superior spine

Upper lateral flexure

Peritoneum (pararectal fossa)

Superior rectal artery

Rectum

Sacro-tuberous ligament

Ischio-rectal fossa

Anal canal

Anus

Third sacral vertebra

Fourth sacral vertebra (cut)

Lower border of piriformis (cut)

Superior rectal artery

Middle lateral flexure

Levator ani

Coccygeus

External sphincter

Rat

FIG. 525.—THE RECTUM FROM BEHIND.

THE IDEA HORRIFIED—AND FASCINATED—ME!

I IMAGINED THE SAME PUNISHMENT MIGHT BEFALL MY LOVED ONES.

BUT WHY SHOULD IT?

The patient had lost his spectacles a few days before hearing about the torture. He had written to Vienna for a new pair and arranged for an officer in the next village to pick them up. But then he heard the "rat story" . . .

IF I FAIL TO PAY THAT OFFICER BACK... MY LOVED ONES WILL BE PUNISHED!

YET HE WAS ALSO CONVINCED OF THE **OPPOSITE!**

EVEN IF I DO PAY HIM BACK... THEY'LL BE PUNISHED ANYWAY!

To avert this danger the Rat Man had to follow a set of bizarre, self-imposed 'instructions', so complicated that they became impossible to follow.

And even Freud got involved in drawing up maps and time-tables!

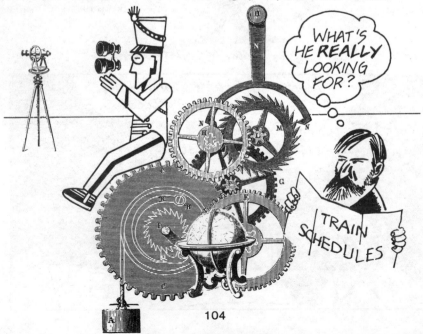

WHAT'S HE **REALLY** LOOKING FOR?

TRAIN SCHEDULES

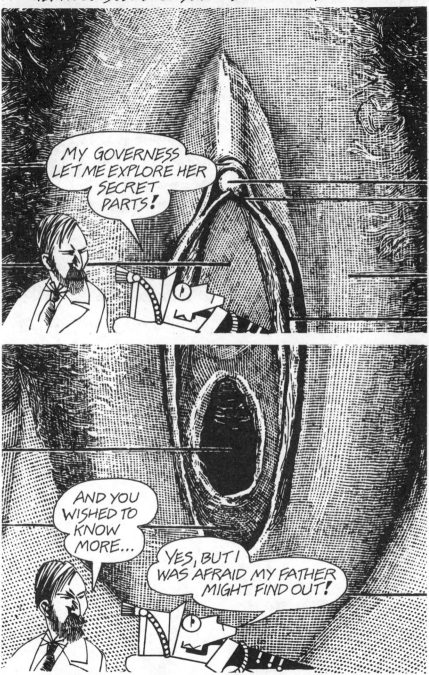

Sexual arousal became linked with punishment and hostility against his father.

This childhood fixation is shown by one of the Rat Man's 'rituals' devised while studying for an exam. He would stay up every night till between midnight and 1 a.m.

THE HOUR WHEN MY FATHER MIGHT APPEAR! READING BECAME IMPOSSIBLE... I WENT TO OPEN THE DOOR TO LET HIM IN...

RETURNING TO THE HALL... I TURNED ON ALL THE LIGHTS...

...UNDRESSED... AND LOOKED AT MY PENIS IN THE MIRROR.

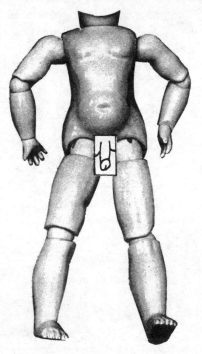

FREUD LEARNED SOMETHING ELSE...

He adopted a new belief to protect a **past** one: that his father would still interfere even after death.

THE RAT MAN'S EARLY SEXUAL DEVELOPMENT WAS ASSOCIATED WITH EXTREME DOUBTS.

WHEN I EXPERIENCED MY FIRST ERECTIONS...I WENT TO COMPLAIN ABOUT THEM TO MY MOTHER. BUT WHY BOTHER? THEY **KNOW** ALL MY THOUGHTS ANYWAY!

His complaint about genital urges suggests a fixation at the anal stage. The stage, in fact, which is **overseen** by the parents!
Most cases of obsessional neurosis can be traced back to anal fixations, which are often related to **sadistic** urges.
That's why the "rat story" obsesses him!

Slowly Freud began to piece together the hidden meaning of the Rat Man's unconscious ideas. For instance . . .

So now he felt obliged to return and replace the stone **exactly** where it had been.

The Rat Man's intentions are reversed. The punishment he fears for others is really what he fears for himself.

Normal behaviour operates in reality and in the present. But the Rat Man's actions do not make sense in the real, here-and-now present, because his sexual anxiety refers to the past.

His actions only make sense as a need to **repeat** something in the past. The neurotic repeats instead of remembering.

THE RAT MAN'S ANALYSIS LASTED 11 MONTHS. HIS NEUROSIS WAS COMPLETELY CLEARED – UNTIL HIS DEATH IN THE FIRST WORLD WAR.

THE PSYCHOANALYTICAL MOVEMENT

Freud attracted followers and pioneer psychoanalysts between 1902-08. These first practitioners formed the **Vienna Psychoanalytical Society**.

The first International Congress was held in Salzburg, April 1908.

Invited to lecture in the USA by Stanley Hall, President of Clark University, Freud set sail in August 1909 with Jung and Ferenczi. On board the **George Washington** Freud finds his cabin-steward reading . . .

FREUD DISLIKED AMERICA...

By 1910 Freud had gained international recognition.
But now he faced struggles within the psychoanalytical movement
itself. Disputes led to splits between Freud and his early followers,
Adler, Stekel, Jung, Rank, etc.

IT IS SOMETIMES SAID THAT THESE SPLITS WERE CAUSED
BY FREUD'S TYRANNICAL AND DOGMATIC PERSONALITY.
BUT AS FREUD TOLD HIS BIOGRAPHER ERNEST JONES...

Let's look briefly at the most famous split of all — between Freud and Jung.

Carl Jung (1875-1961) was a psychiatrist at the Burghölzli mental hospital in Zurich.
He was the first to try out Freud's psychoanalytical methods on psychotic illnesses more severe than neurosis.
Jung was the first to apply the famous term **complex**, and he also devised word-association tests for use in diagnosis.

FREUD WAS VERY IMPRESSED WITH JUNG, AND VICE-VERSA.

JUNG IS LIKE A SON — THE CROWN-PRINCE OF THE MOVEMENT!

It was important to Freud that Jung was an established psychiatrist, not Viennese and not Jewish. Freud told his colleague Karl Abraham...

TOO MANY OF US ARE JEWS... I DON'T WANT PSYCHOANALYSIS TO BECOME A JEWISH NATIONAL AFFAIR!

But even at the start of their friendship Jung admitted his confused feelings about Freud.

MY VENERATION FOR YOU IS SOMETHING LIKE A 'RELIGIOUS CRUSH'...

"Though it does not really bother me, I still feel it is disgusting and ridiculous because of its undeniable erotic undertone. This abominable feeling comes from the fact that as a boy I was the victim of a sexual assault by a man I once worshipped."
From Jung's letter to Freud, 28 Oct. 1907.

Freud's reply was that a "religious crush" might end badly — in rebellion.

"I shall do my best to show you that I am unfit to be an object of worship."
Freud to Jung, 15 Nov. 1907.

This business of being "like father and son" would lead to trouble.
In September 1912 Jung went alone to New York to lecture at Fordham University. He believed he was "defending" Freud. But his criticisms of Freud's basic ideas went pretty deep.

Jung struck at the root of Freud's discovery — at the childhood and sexual origins of neurotic disorders. Freud saw Jung's "independence" as a resistance to the unconscious and a wish to destroy the father.

THINGS WEREN'T GOOD WHEN FREUD AND JUNG NEXT MET FOR A CONFERENCE AT THE PARK HOTEL IN MUNICH IN NOVEMBER 1912.
BUT AFTER A 2-HOUR 'TALKING TO'...

FREUD'S 'LITTLE VICTORY' DIDN'T RESOLVE THE TENSION...BECAUSE AT LUNCH...

JUNG CARRIED HIM TO THE NEXT ROOM.

AND WHEN FREUD CAME TO...

What did Freud mean? Had he ever fainted before?
Yes, once before in 1909 after convincing the teetotaller Jung to celebrate their voyage to the USA with a glass of wine.
And years before that (as he told Ernest Jones) he had similar symptoms in the **same** room of the Park Hotel.

Relations between Freud and Jung grew worse. In his letter of 18 Dec. 1912 Jung blamed Freud for causing the splits in the movement.

By the spring of 1913 Freud had completed a new book, **Totem and Taboo**, which he realized would hasten the split with Jung.
Jung wished to reduce the importance of incest fantasies. In this book Freud expands the significance of the Oedipus complex by tracing it back to the beginnings of human society!

TOTEMISM AND INCEST

The totem is the spirit or ancestor of a tribal clan, usually symbolized by an animal which it is forbidden to harm or kill.

Totemism is linked with **exogamy**: a kinship system which forbids sexual relations between members of the same totem-clan. Incest was thereby outlawed.

WHY IS INCEST PROHIBITED? OBVIOUSLY NOT FOR BIOLOGICAL REASONS – BUT FOR A STRICTLY SOCIAL PURPOSE.

Society can only get started if relations between different families are instituted through sexual laws.

But once a year the totem animal-ancestor is killed and eaten. Ritual grief is followed by wild rejoicing.

What does this yearly ritual murder of the totemic ancestor mean?

Totemism must imply another, deeper myth.

THE PRIMAL MYTH

Darwin suggests that early ape-like humans lived in small hordes consisting of one powerful patriarch and his females.

Freud suggests that rivalry for the females pushed the younger males to kill and eat the old father.

Guilt following this original Oedipal crime led to the tribal totemic laws against murder and incest.

Repression of this primitive Oedipal crime into the unconscious stands at the beginning of all human culture, religion and art.

FREUD WAS SURE HIS THEORY OF SEXUALITY WAS RIGHT.
BUT THAT DOESN'T MEAN HE HAD NO DOUBTS.

Freud realized he needed something better to explain the source of conflict and repression.

This wasn't just a problem of theory but a practical one of being able to treat his patients successfully.

PROBLEMS OF THERAPY

The success of therapy depends upon overcoming the forces which work against therapy. How deep do these 'forces' go? And what are they?

The symptoms expressed by a neurotic can be traced back to repressed, unconscious wishes or impulses.

But what is the therapist to **do** about it? **How can the patient be made conscious of the unconscious**?

So how can analysis make what is unconscious conscious?

Freud made use of something he'd known about since 1895. He had spotted two obstacles which could come between the patient and the doctor. 1) The patient begins to **resist** therapy. Or 2) as in Breuer's treatment of Anna O . . .

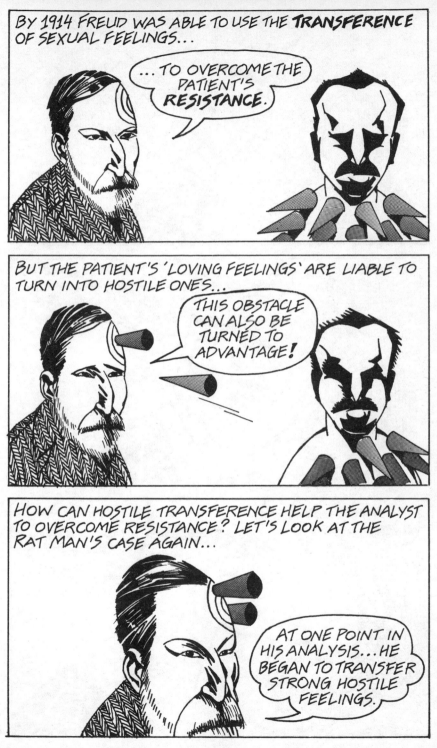

The Rat Man admitted his fear that Freud might punish him for his insults.

So even hostile transference can be important. Why? Because it recreates a 'miniature' neurosis in the present.

Freud said, "The neurotic **repeats** instead of remembering."

He repeats because something unconscious, repressed in the past, puts up a resistance to remembering.

But when he repeats by feeling hostile to Freud in the present, this can **now** be interpreted and turned into actual remembrance.

Only once the unconscious material is in the open (relived as a **second** neurosis during analysis) can it be resolved. This is what Freud called "transference neurosis," which can be cured.

But suppose there is **no** transference? Such cases are more serious.

So long as there is **some** erotic relation (even in fantasy), the problem is treatable.

But what if a transference relation of love or hate can't be made? This means the patient has given up all erotic attachment to people or things. If the patient can't be "reached," the illness is not treatable by the psychoanalytical method of transference.

Freud called the nontreatable or psychotic cases **narcissistic**. What did he mean by that?

THE MYTH OF NARCISSUS

This is another ancient Greek legend about a beautiful youth who fell in love with his own image.

Frustrated because he couldn't possess himself, he faded away and was transformed into the narcissus flower.

NORMAL NARCISSISM

Narcissism is a normal stage of infancy. In building its **ego** (the 'I') the infant searches for its mirror-self.

Normally the infantile narcissistic libido is transferred to objects, that is, to people.

*THERE IS SOME **SELF**-LOVE IN ALL NORMAL ADULT LOVE.*

What about love of self as one would **wish** it to be? Is that normal too?
Yes. Freud called this the EGO-IDEAL.
The ego-ideal is a substitute for the lost narcissism of childhood when I was my **own** ideal.

A strong ego is a protection against falling ill. But, finally, we must begin to love in order not to fall ill. We are sure to fall ill if, because of frustration, we are unable to love.

ABNORMAL NARCISSISM

But what happens if the libido is withdrawn from the world and directed back on the self?

And this **regression** to infantile narcissism can lead to severe psychotic illnesses.

Paranoid delusions of being watched; hearing voices; extreme depression; hypochondria; schizophrenia; megalomania, etc. These are narcissistic psychotic states.

Transference as a second "acted-out" neurosis is impossible because the patient cannot be approached through external erotic attachments.

But a new problem.
Narcissism seems to deny the existence of nonsexual instincts. Even the ego instincts can be included among the libido instincts!

MEANWHILE AN IMMENSE SOCIAL CONFLICT HAD BROKEN OUT.

1914 — THE FIRST WORLD WAR — 1918

FREUD SUPPORTED THE AUSTRO-GERMAN ALLIANCE FOR WHICH HIS SONS WERE FIGHTING.

But his support faded after the first years of war.

"Our civilization has been disfigured by a gigantic hypocrisy. Can we ever again say we are civilized?"

The Austro-German defeat brought galloping inflation in 1919-20. Freud lost all his savings. And he had barely enough patients to earn a living.

Despite hardship, gloom and death-anxiety, Freud kept working on the idea of Narcissism.

MOURNING AND MELANCHOLIA (1915)

Melancholia (as shown in Dürer's engraving, 1514) is an ancient name for psychotic depression.

I FEEL WORTHLESS, GUILTY, SUICIDAL.

WHERE DOES THIS EXAGGERATED GUILT AND SELF-ACCUSATION COME FROM?

FROM MOURNING WHICH HAS GONE BADLY WRONG!

To mourn the loss of a loved one is normal.

But in psychotic depression, the patient's grief conceals unconscious feelings of hate.

Since these feelings cannot be admitted, the lost love object becomes identified with the patient's own ego.

What happens then?

The unconscious hatred, instead of being directed at the lost love **object,** is misdirected against the patient's own self.

Depressive guilt and self-accusation are based on the abnormal regression to infantile narcissism.

Here's an example. A young woman of 19 is admitted to a psychiatric clinic.

IN HOSPITAL SHE ATTEMPTED SUICIDE AND REPEATEDLY MUTILATED **ONE SPOT** ON HER LEFT ARM (WITH RAZOR, SCISSORS, FINGERNAILS).

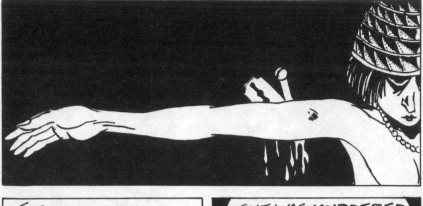

THERAPY BEGAN TO UNRAVEL HER STORY.

I WAS REALLY **CLOSE** TO MY MOTHER...

SHE WAS **MURDERED** BY A SOLDIER...

...AND HORRIBLY MUTILATED... ONLY THE **BIRTHMARK** ON HER LEFT ARM IDENTIFIED HER!

"AFTER MY MOTHER'S DEATH I DEFENDED HER AGAINST THE FAMILY."

THEN, FOR NO APPARENT REASON, SHE GAVE UP HER OLD FRIENDS FOR 'BAD' NEW ONES.

SHE CHANGED RADICALLY AND **BECAME** HER MOTHER! THIS 'ASSUMED PART' OF HERSELF WAS THE TARGET OF REPRESSED HOSTILITY.

BY ACTING 'BAD' SHE WAS ABLE **INDIRECTLY** TO ACCUSE HER MOTHER.

IT'S ALL HER MOTHER'S FAULT!

OF COURSE!

THIS 'NEW IDENTITY' SPARES HER FROM HAVING TO EXPRESS HER OWN NEGATIVE FEELINGS.

This extreme identification is called **INTROJECTION.**
The lost love object is literally embodied or "devoured" by the ego.
The patient regresses to a particular stage of infantile narcissism. This is when the oral stage begins to shade off into the anal stage. During this period, **biting** and **excreting** are dominant, and the infant alternates between love and hate.

BUT A CURE BECAME POSSIBLE WHEN SHE SMASHED ALL THE PANES OF GLASS IN A DOOR.

SHE REMEMBERED AND FINALLY BEGAN TO ACKNOWLEDGE A CONSCIOUS HATRED FOR HER MOTHER.

TOWARDS THE 'DEATH INSTINCT' (1915-1919)

Freud continued his search for a satisfactory theory of **instinctual conflict.**

Since 1895 Freud had assumed that human behaviour was based on **two** contrasting tendencies: on the **pleasure principle** and the **reality principle**. These principles of psychic activity were established in the nervous system.

1. The pleasure principle is primary in the sense of impelling the organism towards immediate, impulsive and wish-fulfilling gratification. It is linked to the unconscious.
2. The reality principle allows the organism to tolerate **delays** or deferments of gratification. This secondary process exercises **thinking**. It permits a certain detachment from sexual impulses and a redirection of energy towards thought, work and play.

The famous mechanism of **sublimation** depends on the reality principle. Sublimation is not — as is popularly supposed — a repression of sexual drives but a redirection of libidinal energy towards a necessary adaptation to reality.

Freud now recognized that the pleasure and reality principles are not really antagonistic to one another, since both aim at the **discharge of tension**. Pleasure is the psychic result of discharging an amount of excitation, stimulus or tension which arises within the organism. The reality principle is only a delayed, modified process of attaining the same aim — which is pleasure.

ALL BEHAVIOUR IS IN THE SERVICE OF TENSION REDUCTION.

BUT JUST A MINUTE...
IF INCREASES OF TENSION
ARE UNPLEASANT...

AND RELIEF FROM
EXCITATION IS PLEASANT...

WHAT ABOUT BEHAVIOUR WHICH CONTRADICTS THIS?
WHAT ABOUT SELF-INJURING BEHAVIOUR SUCH AS
MASOCHISM?

AND WHAT ABOUT THE WARTIME CASES OF "SHELL-SHOCK"?

BUT THE CURIOUS THING WAS THAT THE PATIENT'S DREAMS **REPEATED** THE TERRIFYING TRAUMA.

UNPLEASANT TENSION IS KEPT CONSTANT THROUGH REPETITION.

AND HERE'S ANOTHER EXAMPLE OF REPETITION WHICH FREUD NOTICED.

FREUD WATCHED HIS GRANDSON, AGED $1\frac{1}{2}$, AT PLAY.

HE WAS VERY ATTACHED TO HIS MOTHER.

SHE LEFT HIM FOR A FEW HOURS EVERY DAY. HE DIDN'T COMPLAIN BUT INVENTED A GAME.

HE WAS REPEATING THE DISAPPEARANCE AND RETURN OF HIS MOTHER.

BUT THE QUESTION FREUD NOW ASKED WAS: HOW DOES THE REPETITION OF AN UNPLEASANT EXPERIENCE FIT IN WITH THE PLEASURE PRINCIPLE?

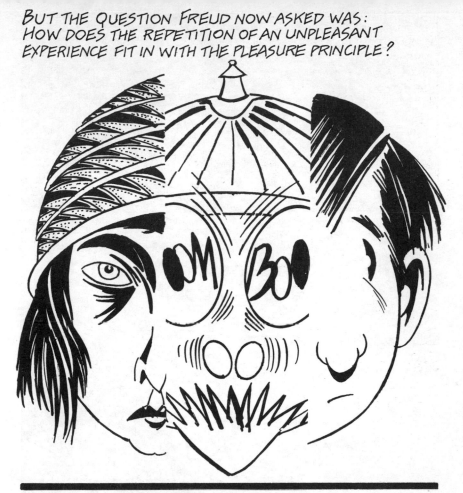

Freud named this puzzling tendency to relive unpleasant or traumatic situations **repetition-compulsion.**

1. An unpleasant surprise always precedes the need to repeat.
2. Normally it is **anxiety** which prepares us to expect danger.
3. Sometimes the psyche suffers a shock or fright for which it is not prepared.
    In such cases, it is not anxiety which produces a traumatic neurosis. In fact, anxiety is what usually protects us against fright or fright-neurosis.
4. So this is the secret of repetition-compulsion. It creates retrospective anxiety in the psyche.
    In other words, the painful memory is relived again and again, until a sufficient defence has been built up "after the event."

This is described in Freud's **Beyond the Pleasure Principle** (1920). But it goes further.

149

SUCH EVIDENCE NOW LED FREUD TO PROPOSE ANOTHER INSTINCT— A DEATH INSTINCT!

The Death Instinct or THANATOS
(Greek for death)

SALMON STRUGGLE UPSTREAM TO RETURN...

...TO SPAWN...

...TO DIE...

...NOT JUST ANY KIND OF DEATH...BUT A HIGHLY SPECIFIC ONE!

The organism defends itself against all threats of death which are not **appropriate** to it.

Paradoxically, the death instinct can serve to **prolong** life.

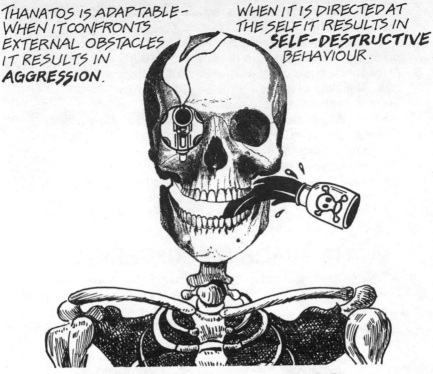

THANATOS IS ADAPTABLE—
WHEN IT CONFRONTS
EXTERNAL OBSTACLES
IT RESULTS IN
AGGRESSION.

WHEN IT IS DIRECTED AT
THE SELF IT RESULTS IN
SELF-DESTRUCTIVE BEHAVIOUR.

The Life Instinct or EROS
(Greek god of Love)

Individual life moves towards a 'natural' death. But the survival of the species does not depend on the individual. The sexual life-instinct which governs the reproductive cells guarantees biological survival.

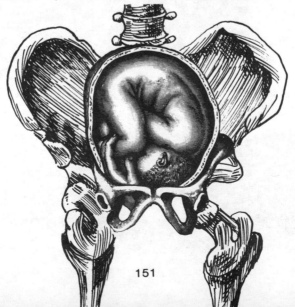

1. The aim of mental activity is to **reduce** tensions provoked either by instinctual or by external excitation.
2. The nervous system of an organism is regulated by a **constancy principle** — a conservative tendency to **stability**.
3. An instinct is therefore the urge inherent in all organic life to restore an **earlier** state of things.
   But how far does this conservative trend go?
4. Since all living matter is made up of non-living, inorganic matter, then perhaps there is an instinct beyond the pleasure principle which aims to return to a state of inorganic inertia.
5. The compulsion to repeat is an instinctual regressive principle which aims to get back to a condition totally devoid of all energy — **death**.

THE AIM OF ALL LIFE IS DEATH.

THE YEARS OF SUFFERING

1920: Freud's 'Sunday child' Sophie dies. She was 26.

1923: Freud's favourite grandson (Sophie's child) dies aged 4½.

That same month, April 1923, Freud was operated on for cancer of the jaw and palate. The first of 33 operations!

The whole upper jaw and palate on the right side were removed. For the last 16 years Freud often suffered agonizing pain. His speech and hearing were affected and eating was difficult.

A prosthesis (a sort of huge denture) had to be designed to shut off the mouth from the nasal cavity.

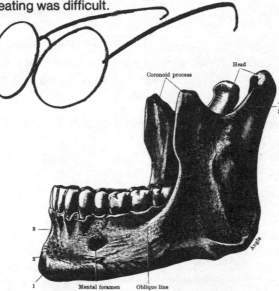

Freud's daughter Anna was his nurse till his death.

Freud did not really come up with a satisfactory answer to an old question which had long bothered him: where does repression come from? Where do we find a "nonsexual" instinct capable of repressing a sexual one—which can lead to neurotic conflict?

Let's go back a bit.

Till now, Freud had assumed that neurosis must arise from unresolved conflicts between conscious (self-) perception and repressed unconscious desires. But he couldn't explain how the repression happened in the first place.

He had also assumed that the ego's "self-preservative" instincts were limited to hunger, thirst and sexual reproduction. But hunger and thirst are not enough to preserve the self; and reproduction is typical of all species and is not specifically individual. We're stuck!

But let's make an imaginative leap...

Let's suppose—to put it simply—that the ego's main problem is to preserve its sense of its own safety, responsibility, and respectability. Freud realized that this continuous effort by the ego to preserve its integrity was the basis of repression, banishing from awareness unconscious contents that could not be acknowledged. This means that repression was just one device in the more general defence of self.

If repression presupposes "something" which represses, then it must be either the ego itself or a split-off aspect of the ego which is responsible for the defensive action of repression.

Therefore, repression comes from the ego. Repression is ego-defencive. Defence against what? Against defects in the development of a mature ego. Anxiety is the proper human signal of weaknesses in the ego. And, of course, a strong or weak ego will depend on the history of the whole personality since childhood.

It becomes clear that human personality has several dynamic features with specific internal and structural roles.

In 1923 Freud proposed a new dynamic model of the mind.

THE EGO, THE ID AND THE SUPER-EGO

THE ID

The ID (Latin for 'it') is the primitive, unconscious basis of the psyche dominated by primary urges.

The psyche of a newborn child is primarily ID.

But contact with the external world modifies part of the ID.

Perception of this difference is what begins to differentiate the EGO.

Ego development is imprinted by the instinctual structure of the libido (mouth, anus, genitals).

In other words, self-awareness and bodily activity develop together.

THE EGO

Freud gives the ego several important functions.

1. The ego is guide in reality. It can adapt or change.
2. Conscious perceptions belong to the ego. This is an aspect of the ego turned towards external reality.
3. But the ego also acts as an inhibiting agency. This is another aspect of the ego which is turned internally and functions unconsciously. For instance, the ego's **repression** of the id is unconscious. This is one of the ego's defence functions. These functions are all unconscious.

Here is one example of the ego's defence mechanism.

A MAN 'SAFELY' GRATIFIES AN OEDIPAL IMPULSE BY MARRYING A WOMAN WHO LOOKS LIKE HIS MOTHER.

THE SUPER-EGO

The super-ego is not just 'conscience.' It is the heir to the Oedipus complex. Here's how it works.

THE INFANT FEELS DEEP HOSTILITY TOWARDS ITS PARENTS, WHICH IT CANNOT EXPRESS...

PARTLY BECAUSE OF LOVE, PARTLY FEAR!

SO THE INFANT PROJECTS ITS AGGRESSION ON TO THEM...

WHICH SEEMS REFLECTED BACK AS EXAGGERATED STRICTNESS...

As the Oedipal impulses are repressed and disappear, their place is taken by the super-ego.
The super-ego is introjected parental authority. It is the result of a defensive effort which prohibits the expression of Oedipal wishes.

Freud turned the conventional view of morality and conscience upside-down!
It is not our strict moral idea which prevents aggressive behaviour. Rather, we have a moral idea **because** we renounce aggression.

What happens to religion? Freud discussed this in **The Future of an Illusion** (1928).

BELIEFS SHAPED BY WISHES CAN'T BE GOOD FOR ANYONE!

Freud was an enemy of all religions. He had no hope for "conscience" based on a repressed part of the personality. He placed his faith in reason and scientific analysis.

The First World War seemed like an awful proof of the struggle between the Life and Death instincts within civilization.
In **Civilization and its Discontents** (1930) Freud asked what the value of civilization is.

Humans may seek pleasure instinctually. But they will actually spend more effort on avoiding pain. Reality provides far more opportunities for experiencing pain than pleasure. So most people will sacrifice pleasure if civilization, in return, can provide them with less suffering.

BUT THE BIG QUESTION IS THIS...

WHO GAINS MOST FROM CIVILIZATION?

The work which makes civilization possible is supplied by a suppressed majority of people who share too little of its wealth. On this, Freud agreed with Marx.

Freud asked himself another question. How do people **identify** themselves as members of a group or society?
Libido-attachment to an object can take place on a mass scale.
Individuals put one and the same object in the place of the super-ego.
They identify themselves with one another in their ego.

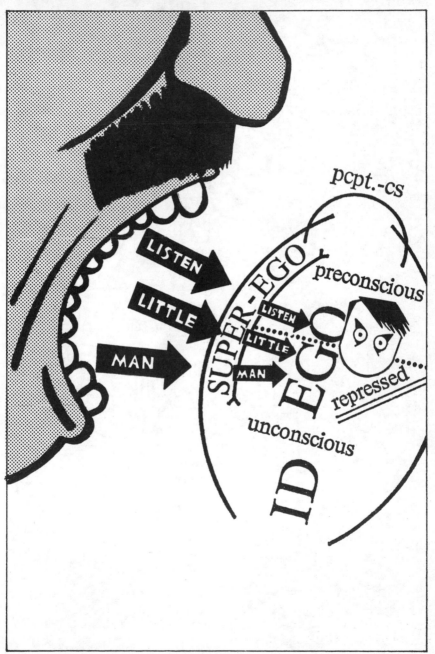

But suppose the super-ego is handed over to one **leader**?
This produces a very dangerous kind of mass "falling in love"!
Which is what happened in Germany in the '30s!

In Berlin, May 1933, the Nazis burn books by Freud and many other great modern thinkers.

Freud was wrong! The Nazis would have gassed and incinerated him too in one of their death-camps— as in fact happened to millions of other Jews, including Freud's own sisters.

March 1938: the Nazis take over Austria. Nazi S.A. men invade Freud's home searching for valuables. Freud's 'Old Testament' frown frightens them away.
Freud's daughter Anna was detained by the Gestapo a whole day.

June 1938: Freud and his family emigrate to London, England.

Freud worked on, despite his worsening cancer, until his death **Sept. 23, 1939**.

LITTLE DICTIONARY

Based on Charles Rycroft's useful
A Critical Dictionary of Psychoanalysis .

ABREACTION: process of releasing repressed emotion by reliving in imagination the original experience.

AFFECT: feeling or emotion attached to ideas, idea-clusters or objects.

AGGRESSION: in Freud's later writings a derivative of the Death Instinct, contrasted to libido, sex or the Life Instinct, Eros. Opinions differ whether aggression is a basic instinctual drive or whether it provides the ego with energy to overcome obstacles in the way of satisfying self-assertive drives.

CATHEXIS: accumulation or quantity of mental energy attaching to some idea, memory or object.

COMPLEX: cluster of ideas (and often memories of real or imaginary experiences) associated with powerful emotions which become buried by the process of repression in the unconscious part of mind and exert a dynamic effect on behaviour. Can sometimes emerge partly or wholly into the conscious mind, although it is the job of repression to prevent this.
Freud recognized only two: the **Oedipus** (or Oedipal) and **Castration complexes.**

Oedipus complex: emerges during the phase of ego development between the ages of 3 and 5 and can later be responsible for much unconscious guilt. Persons fixated at the Oedipal level show it in many ways, for example, by choosing sexual partners who resemble their parent(s).

Castration complex: Oedipal rivalry with fathers causes castration anxiety in males. Girls and women cannot suffer this male anxiety. But they too can feel 'castrated,' wish to prove they possess an adequate (symbolic) substitute for the penis; or feel anxiety toward whatever organ, object or activity is a penis-equivalent for them. The origin of this complex is related by Freud to penis-envy. Much criticized by feminists.

DEATH INSTINCT or THANATOS: different from aggressive wish to kill others; rather, the individual's own innate self-destructive drive. Freud distinguished 2 kinds of instincts. Sexual ones (Eros) which perpetually attempt and achieve the renewal of life. Another which seeks to lead what is living to death. Not supported by any known biological principle.

DEFENCE: negatively, its function is to protect the ego which may be threatened by anxieties from (a) the id, super-ego or outside world, (b) bad conscience or super-ego threats, (c) real dangers. Positively, defence mechanisms are used by the ego to channel or control the forces which may lead to neurosis. Defense acts as a compromise between wish and reality. The ego modifies the id's urges for immediate gratification and allows disguised satisfaction. The point of any defensive compromise is to keep the conflicts it resolves out of conscious awareness.

DISPLACEMENT: shifting of affect from one mental image to another to which it does not really belong, as in dreams.

DREAM WORK: (a) the function of dreams is to preserve sleep by representing wishes as fulfilled which would otherwise wake the dreamer. (b) The manifest content of dreams starts from various sensory experiences received during sleep, plus worries of the previous day and recent past life. (c) Latent repressed wishes from the unconscious attach themselves to this content. To evade censorship and prevent the sleeper from waking, these latent wishes modify or disguise their content. This modification taking place in the unconscious is the dream work.

EGO, ID, SUPER-EGO: structural concepts; 'places' (topography) within the psychic apparatus; but not actually 'located' in the brain.
Psyche (mental apparatus) begins as

unorganized id ("everything present at birth") out of which a structured ego develops. Infancy progresses through the libido phases (oral, anal, phallic, Oedipal) in which the id's sources and forms of sexual pleasure change. Paralleling these phases, the ego develops functions enabling the individual to master impulses, operate independently of parental figures and control environment.

Part of the ego develops the self-critical activities of the super-ego which depend on the introjection of parental figures. The severity of the super-ego partly derives from the violence of the subject's own unconscious feelings in early infancy. The energies of the super-ego may also derive from the id: the self-attacking tendency of the super-ego provides an outlet for the subject's aggressive impulses. Super-ego contains both the infantile past and a higher level of the ego's self-reflective functions.

FIXATION: failure to progress adequately through the stages of libidinal development can cause fixation: attachment to objects appropriate to those earlier infantile stages. Fixated persons suffer frustrating wastes of energy because of their over-investment in past objects.

GUILT: specifically neurotic guilt, i.e., experiences of feeling guilty which cannot be explained by real violations of the patient's conscious values. Result of conflicts between super-ego and infantile sexual and aggressive wishes. Expressions of aggressive feeling taken out on oneself through the super-ego's 'moral' condemnation. Defences to reduce anxiety can also reduce guilt.

HYSTERIA: illness once considered as either (a) physical in origin, or (b) in which physical evidence of illness was absent. Since Charcot, and especially psychoanalysis, seen as neurotic forms of behaviour in which the physical symptoms (e.g., convulsions, paralysis, disturbances of sight, hearing, etc.) derive from psychological malfunctions. Hysteria was diagnosed as a purely female or 'uterine' disease. Freud rejected this but kept the idea that it was somehow connected to sexuality. The 2 recognized forms of hysteria are: (a) **conversion-hysteria,** a form of psychoneurosis in which symptoms appear as physical complaints, as in Anna O's case; and (b) **anxiety-hysteria,** now

known as **phobia,** as in Little Hans's case.

The symptom of phobia is extreme neurotic anxiety experienced in certain situations (e.g., claustrophobia, anxiety in enclosed spaces) or when faced with certain objects (e.g., spiders, snakes or horses, as in Hans's case).

A person with a phobic character has the habit of dealing with situations that are likely to cause anxiety or conflict either (a) by rigidly avoiding them, or (b) by seeking and taking pleasure in activities which are dangerous and normally arouse anxiety in others.

IMPULSE: in neurology refers to the wave of electrical charge passing along a nerve fibre. Freud also described movements of psychic energy in this way: instinctual impulses 'travel' from the id along channels to the ego where these are either (a) discharged in action, (b) inhibited, (c) directed by defence mechanisms or (d) sublimated.

INHIBITION: a process is inhibited if it is 'switched off' by the operation of some other process. So fear can inhibit sexual desire, etc. Inhibiting agencies are usually the ego or super-ego; the inhibited process is usually an instinctual impulse. Inhibition can be seen as a symptom.

INSTINCT: innate biological drive to action; has (a) a biological source and (b) a supply of energy; (c) its aim is satisfaction which (d) it seeks in objects. Failure to find satisfaction or objects causes frustration and increases of instinctual tension experienced as pain. This pain (according to the Pleasure Principle) must seek relief and leads to the triggering of defence mechanisms to reduce tension. Anxiety is the ego's way of reacting to instinctual tension which stimulates its defences. Freud claimed an instinct can undergo 4 changes: (a) repression, (b) sublimation, (c) turning against the self (using the self as an instinctual object), (d) reversal (into its opposite, e.g., replacing an active role by a passive one).

INTROJECTION: process by which relationship with an object (out there) is replaced by one with an imagined mental object (in here). Super-ego is formed by introjection of parental/authority figures. Introjection is both a defence (against anxiety caused by separation) and a normal development (helps the subject to become autonomous).

LIBIDO: sexual desire; vital impulse or energy. Hypothetical form of mental energy flowing into psychic processes, structures and objects. The proposed source of libido is the body or id; exists as related to specific erotogenic zones or libidinized psychic structures.
Freud first thought of libido as energy attached to specific sexual instincts. Later, narcissistic libido was seen as invested in the ego, i.e., libido originally attached to parent objects, because of frustration, becomes attached to the ego. Self-love, self-awareness increases as attachment to parents decreases. Ego, by this, becomes its own object.

NEUROSIS: originally a disease of the nerves; later describing diseases due to functional disturbances of the nervous system unaccompanied by structural changes. Freud's discovery is that neurosis is a disorder of the personality, not a disease of the nervous system; a conflict phenomenon involving the thwarting of some fundamental instinctual urge.
There are several types of neuroses: due to past causes; present sexual habits; shock; symptoms as character traits; psychosomatic. Example: **obsessional neurosis.** Obsessions are ideas or groups of ideas persistently intruding upon the patient's consciousness involuntarily despite the recognition of their abnormality. Major symptoms are obsessional thoughts and compulsive ritual behaviour. Such thoughts differ from normal ones because the patient experiences them as bizarre, obscene, unspontaneous, repetitive; and behaviour is also repetitive, stereotyped, bound. Obsessional neurosis centres on regression to the anal-sadistic stage and ambivalence toward introjected parents.

PSYCHE: originally the 'soul'; psychologically, the mind, mental apparatus. Usually contrasted with **soma,** the body, or general physical factors.

PSYCHIATRY: branch of medicine treating mental illnesses. Unlike **psychoanalysis** (the theory and therapeutic treatment of neuroses) psychiatry (a) treats illnesses of known physical origin, e.g., senility, mental deficiency, etc.; (b) employs different techniques such as electro-shock therapy and drugs; and (c) tends to regard mental illness as due to physical factors, known or unknown.
Psychology is defined as 'science of mind' or today 'science of behaviour' and has many specialized branches: experimental, social, animal, industrial, etc. Psychoanalysis may be regarded as one such branch.

PSYCHOSIS: used by both psychiatry and psychoanalysis to describe mental illnesses which may lead to total loss of reality and control over behaviour; contrasted to neurosis in which the patient's sanity is never in doubt.
Psychiatry distinguishes between organic psychosis due to demonstrable organic disease and functional psychoses without apparent organic origin. The 3 functional psychoses recognized by both branches are schizophrenia, manic-depressive psychosis and paranoia. Psychoanalysis considers psychosis as a narcissistic disorder inaccessible to treatment because transference cannot be formed.

REGRESSION: as a result of fixation, reversion to expressive channels of libidinal and ego development belonging to infantile stages. Also a defensive process seeking to avoid anxiety by a return to earlier patterns of behaviour: not a viable defence since regression compels the individual to re-experience anxiety appropriate to the regressed stage.
Free association can be seen as a 'controlled' therapeutic form of regression useful in the working out of neurosis.

REPRESSION: defence mechanism by which unacceptable impulse or idea is rendered unconscious. Mental process arising from conflicts between the Pleasure and Reality Principles. Impulses, memories and painful emotions arising from such conflicts, and thrust into the unconscious, still remain active, indirectly influencing experience and behaviour, producing neurotic symptoms and also determining (normal) dreams. Ego development depends on repression.

RESISTANCE: opposition to the analyst's interpretation during the psychoanalytical process of making unconscious patterns conscious.

SEXUALITY: Freud upset traditional ideas of sex by asserting that (a) adult sexual behaviour has infantile origins (oral, anal erotism and component instincts) which contribute to the development of the adult sexual instinct and personality as a whole; that (b) infantile and adult sexual drives influence non-sexual behaviour as filtered through symbolization and sublimation.

to repression. Some things can be easily recalled; others, such as some fantasies, wishes, painful memories, exist but can only become conscious after the removal of specific resistances. On the evidence of the latter Freud bases his hypothesis of a dynamic unconscious.

SUBLIMATION: psychic development by which instinctual energies are discharged in non-instinctual forms of behaviour. Displacement of such energy to ones of less instinctual interest; desexualized or deaggressified emotion; liberation of activity from demands of instinctual tension. Can perhaps best be understood negatively: e.g. a patient who before his neurotic breakdown had an inquiring ('devouring') mind now turned to over-eating (oral regression); or one with previous intellectual curiosity turned to voyeurism. These examples suggest that the instincts available for sublimation are the pregenital component instincts. Sublimation depends on unconscious

SYMBOLIZATION: "only what is repressed is symbolized; only what is repressed needs to be symbolized," Ernest Jones (1916); and ego development depends on sublimation.

SYMPTOM : effect of a compromise between repressed wish and repressing agency (ego, super-ego). Symptom-formation in neurosis shares the characteristics of normal dream work.

TRANSFERENCE: displacement on to the analyst of feelings, ideas, which derive from the introjected figures or objects acquired in the patient's past life. The analyst's detachment (refusal to 'play along' or respond to the patient's expectations) creates a novel or 'second neurosis' which it is possible to interpret as the patient behaving as though the analyst were a father, mother, brother, etc. This is the crucial **transference-neurosis** in which the conflict is worked through, unconscious patterns becoming conscious to the patient.

UNCONSCIOUS: can there be mental processes of which the subject is unaware? Are unconscious mental processes, by definition, self-contradictory? These are crucial questions/criticisms of psychoanalysis. Freud responds by assuming 2 kinds of unconscious processes: those which can become conscious easily; others subject

FURTHER READING

BOOKS BY FREUD

The best introduction to Freud is Freud himself. But two warnings. Don't start with *An Outline of Psychoanalysis* (1938): it is not an elementary work as the title suggests. Second, Freud's writings are summaries of his work as it stood to date. He kept revising and never really supplied a final, complete 'system'.

Here are some basic books which may help beginners to start reading Freud for themselves.

A collection of Freud's writings selected by his daughter Anna Freud, available in Penguin Books, *The Essentials of Psychoanalysis* contains the seminal pieces and provides a comprehensive view of his central concepts.

Freud's case studies on Dora, Little Hans, Hysteria, etc., are recommended because they combine good story-telling with analytic technique. These are available in paperback editions in the Freud Pelican Library, Penguin Books, or the reader can consult the 24-volume Standard Edition of *The Complete Works of Sigmund Freud* (Hogarth Press, London). Appreciation of the case studies should prepare the reader to try Freud's *The Interpretation of Dreams* and *The Psychopathology of Everyday Life*, available in the paperback series mentioned. Alternatively, the reader might prefer Freud's *A General Introduction to Psychoanalysis* (28 lectures to lay persons, 1915-17) and *New Introductory Lectures on Psychoanalysis* (1932-36), both in Penguin Books.

BOOKS ON FREUD

Ernest Jones' biography *The Life and Work of Sigmund Freud* (Pelican Biographies, Penguin Books, 1974) is still the classic one. It has its biases, but has the advantage of being written by someone who knew Freud and was personally involved in the foundation of psychoanalysis. It is gripping reading and introduces all the major psychoanalytic father-figures.

David Stafford-Clarke's *What Freud Really Said* (Penguin Books) provides a good, clear and brief introduction. For an intellectual assessment of Freud's ideas, Barry Richards' *Images of Freud: Responses to Psychoanalysis* (J.M. Dent and Sons, 1989) is reader-friendly and excellent. Richard Wollheim's *Freud* (Fontana Modern Masters) is a classic introduction which emphasizes the importance of Freud's theory of mind, but is perhaps a little difficult for the beginner.

R.E. Fancher's *Psychoanalytic Psychology* (W.W. Norton & Co., New York) gives a clear account of Freudian theory as a scientific product. Alternatively, Paul Kline's *Fact and Fantasy in Freudian Theory* (Methuen, London) sets out to invalidate Freud's claim to science from an experimental viewpoint.

EXTENDED READING

Norman O. Brown's *Life Against Death* (Sphere Books) provides the reader with a stimulating and controversial application of psychoanalysis to the meaning of culture and history.

Another classic of the 1960s, Herbert Marcuse's *Eros and Civilization* (Sphere Books, 1969) combines liberal Marxism and Freudian theory in an examination of politics, society and culture.

Feminist criticisms of Freud have often been hostile, particularly in the U.S. Juliet Mitchell's *Psychoanalysis and Feminism* (Penguin Books) should be consulted for an assessment of the feminist misreadings of Freud by the former gurus of sexual politics, Friedan, Millett, and others. Mitchell's interpretation is balanced, positive and radically feminist. An important book, but not easy.

Richard Appignanesi, born Montreal, Canada, in 1940, came to the U.K. in 1967 to complete his D.Phil. in Art History at the University of Sussex. He was a founder member of the Writers & Readers Publishing Cooperative and the originating art editor of the Beginners Series for which he also wrote *Lenin for Beginners*. He is the author of a fiction trilogy, *Italia Perversa: Stalin's Orphans, The Mosque* and *Destroying America*, and is currently Research Associate at King's College, London.

Oscar Zarate, born Buenos Aires, 1942, was an art director in several advertising agencies there until 1970. He settled in London in 1971 to become a freelance illustrator of comic strips and graphic novels. His works include: *Lenin for Beginners, Fatlips* – a children's book with Arnold Wesker, the graphic novels of Shakespeare's *Othello*, Marlowe's *Dr Faustus, Geoffrey the Tube Train and the Fat Comedian* with Alexei Sayle, *A Small Killing* with Alan Moore, and he has several works-in-progress, *Fly Blues* with Carlos Sampayo and children's books.

ECOLOGY FOR BEGINNERS
Stephen Croall and William Rankin

Fully revised and updated, this is a fascinating but disquieting portrait of our beleaguered earth which points to the kind of sustainable alternatives that might save it.

'The author and artist have brought together a quite extraordinary range of material in an original way and in many respects this is just the handbook that many of us have been looking for.'

New Society, reviewing the first edition

DARWIN FOR BEGINNERS
Jonathan Miller and Borin Van Loon

In this classic bestseller, Jonathan Miller unravels Darwin's life and contribution to biology and traces the path from his scientific predecessors to modern genetics.

'The story of Darwin's life could not be told better or more dramatically.'

Lord Longford, *Books and Bookmen*

'Miller and Van Loon have brought to life an important chapter of scientific history . . . I think this should count as a real achievement.'

New Scientist

EINSTEIN FOR BEGINNERS
Joseph Schwartz and Michael McGuinness

Amusing, irreverent, sophisticated and highly accessible, **Einstein for Beginners** has become established internationally as one of the best introductions to Einstein's life and thought.

'The presentation of Einstein's discoveries is little short of inspired.'

The Washington Post